Pillow Thoughts III
Mending the Mind

Pillow Thoughts III
Mending the Mind

Courtney Peppernell

Andrews McMeel
PUBLISHING®

Acknowledgments

Publishing a book is never easy. It takes time, dedication, and hard work. I'm so blessed to have an amazing support network around me. James, you never fail to get things done when we need them done—we are such a solid pair. Emma, you have been here from the start of this series and always offer me honest and infallible advice in the development stages. Lindsay, you are not just my dear friend but also amazing in the work you do for our social media and the Pillow Thoughts brand; I am eternally grateful to you. To everyone at Andrews McMeel Publishing, especially Kirsty, Fred, Patty, Elizabeth, Holly, and Diane, I am so grateful every day for your belief in me and your dedication to this series. To my family—Mum, Dad, Nick, Judy and Simon, and Ma—your support never waivers, and I couldn't do this without you.

To my little team at home, Rhian, Jay, Stacey, Zach, Briana, Hero, and Dakota—thank you for always believing in me and supporting the books. I love our lives together; we're a family!

Lastly, to my readers—you've taken this little Jellyfish further than I thought it would go. Thank you for everything; I can't wait to see where we go next. May it be an adventure together.

Courtney

Twitter: @CourtPeppernell
Instagram: @courtneypeppernell
Email: courtney@pepperbooks.org

Before we begin, I'd like to remind you of a story.
Once upon a time, there was a jellyfish called
You.

You had ventured with heart

You had repaired the cracks

You had filled the holes

and You had healed the heart.

Now You must seek answers and find

wisdom within the mind

I hate to spoil the ending

But You

can heal minds.

Table of Thoughts

If your mind is on someone

I keep myself distracted all throughout the day

with coffee and books

and things that make me drift away

But always between every heartbeat

no matter what it is I do

I am constantly thinking of you

I've been thinking about you. Writing out text messages without pressing send. I've been dreaming about kissing you, one day when I have courage, to tell you I want to be more than just friends.

When we met, there was a pull. Like two magnets unsure of the way we wanted to feel. You told me that night you were afraid of fireworks but loved colors in the sky. And all week I've been wondering if I could be a color you'd want to know.

In the mornings, I think about holding your hand, drinking coffee in bookstores, and keeping that heart of yours forever. But then it is night, and I imagine pulling off your dress and falling into sheets, your thighs shaking and my lips making you weak.

I've never wanted perfect. I love messy handwriting, days that feel like they are blurred into one. I love notes left on windowsills and lipstick stains on coffee mugs. I love piling into bed late at night with socks still on. I love passion. Show me your love; talk about your dreams. There is beauty in the chaos of living.

It doesn't have to be two in the morning to think about you. I think about you when I am filing through the moments of my day. And yet at 2 a.m. when I am thinking about you, I am also pretending what it would feel like to be in your arms.

I spent the night sitting cross-legged on the front lawn, wondering how many times a star would be born before dawn. The sky opened and I watched a star streak through, burning quickly, rushing toward the earth. Such beauty in vastness, like you, when you wear your hair the way you do.

I wish for someone to look at me and lose the next thing they were going to say.

Surely you must know

How much

I love you so

Of every life I've ever lived,

I am sure somewhere

At some point

I was thinking about you

I exist between my faith in her and my loyalty to us

I grow with the knowledge that she grows beside me

Loyalty isn't only when it suits you. There is no such thing as loyal during the week but on the weekend it's someone new you seek. When you are loyal, you are loyal for life. There are no excuses. Either you commit or you don't.

For some it is your smile or eyes they notice first. They talk about how beautiful your hair is, how words roll off your tongue in elegance. But for me, it is more in the way you hold yourself. Even after everything, you hold yourself in a way that says, "I am still here; I survived."

The grass isn't always greener on the other side. In fact, that grass has been tendered and grown by someone else. Just because your front lawn is withering doesn't mean you can destroy someone else's.

First Date

My dress got caught in your car door, and the more you
tried to fix the tear, the more the hem unraveled. My cheeks
were flushed, thinking if only I had worn jeans, but you were
laughing, talking about a time you had split your pants in
front of an entire room. You asked if I wanted to go home,
but I said no, because your smile had made everything light
again. We didn't go to the restaurant; instead, we got takeout
from a pastry shop nearby, and you took me to a bridge,
just east of where you learned how to fly. We watched the
runway, metal birds taking flight and landing, and I asked if
your favorite thing was to be in the air. You said it was, until
tonight, before you knew someone could steal your heart,
even with just a dress tear.

It is not a chore

my want for you

darling your love for me

I do adore

She wanted a love so loyal people would whisper how lucky she was in the halls. She wanted a love to cherish with everything she had, from her soul, to her heart, existing in every bone.

Here I was, staring at the snow falling outside, ready to give up on meeting anybody new. Yet you walked inside, hung your coat on the back of the booth, shook the sleet from your hair, and I tried not to look your way, tried not to stare. Now here we are, your feet up on the dashboard of my car, talking about the moment we were ready to give up on love. How all the moments we've had since then have all been together. How through everything, we somehow make each other better.

There will come a day when I am not wondering how you are.
When all the parts of us we shared will just become memories
to store away. I won't feel a tightness in my chest when I see
a picture of you, or wonder if it's you when my phone rings.
Maybe I'll even understand why my first love is the one that
seems to haunt me.

I don't think about you when I'm lonely; I think about you when I'm doing the things I love. And I don't know what makes me feel sadder, the fact that I miss you when I can't share my day or that I'm still thinking about you late at night.

What name do you want to forget?

Why is it keeping you awake at 4 a.m.?

I deleted all the photos

I took down the wall hangings at home

I packed up all your things

I deleted your number from my phone

But here I am still thinking about you

every morning I drive to work

Because we used to get coffee and listen

to the radio

And now everyone is telling me to get

the train instead

Because I can't let go of all our habits

and it's breaking me, I know

When the music slows

and the world

     feels like

it's standing still

It's you I want to be with

to love you fiercely

     like I know I will

My mother said I could

fall for anyone

That love has no boundaries

That love could be as

endless as the sky

and as beautiful as the sea

So why did I have to fall

for someone

who didn't fall for me

I've been cleaning my house all day. Sometimes cleaning makes me feel like I'm removing all the dust from my life. I've been thinking while I clean. About people and places and the types of souls I want in my life. That's all we are, aren't we, just souls who are sometimes kind and sometimes cruel and almost always complicated. I'm healthy. I've met someone. She's a torch in the cave that feels dark.

> I need to clean up my life in the same way I've cleaned up my house.

Even after all this hurt, and the mess of being together, the saddest part was not the tears or the constant shutting of doors. It's that this was the best we could do.

She's not mine yet

I don't think you can belong to someone

Anymore

But how I would love her

If she could be mine

I have good days

And bad days

And on both

I am thinking of you

It's your birthday, and you deserve all the happiness there is.
You deserve balloons and cake and the sun to shine all day.
You deserve love and well wishes and for things to go your
way. You deserve promise and to be all you can be. It's your
birthday, and I hope you wish for me.

It's never about making

my whole world about you

And I don't want you to make me yours

But I want to share your world

Show you mine

I hope you want that too

I've been thinking about the younger me. What I would have told her now. How as you get older there are more and more responsibilities. Like laundry and bills and car registrations. Like renewing phone plans and working long hours and trying to navigate priorities. Younger me would have laughed, said that's not life. But it is life. Life hits you hard. It doesn't matter if you're ready for it or not; it still happens.

But you grow into it.

I'd tell her, don't worry, you get there eventually.

If you are giving your attention to someone, they should be giving theirs back to you. If they're not, it's either because yours is unwanted or they're just not available.

I am drunk on the idea of us together,

huddled under blankets, talking for hours.

I am caught up in the idea of taking you

on a date and bringing you flowers.

You are all kinds of wonderful

filled with memories

that have made you strong

and brave

I get butterflies every time

someone says your name

It took me such a long time to be myself

So now the only person I want to be with

is someone who wouldn't ever want me to be

anybody else

The highway moved past us in fleeting images of blurred lines and trees.

"Do you think about finding love?" she asked.

I glanced in the rearview mirror, the mountains behind us.

"Not often, why?"

She played with her hair, curling it between her fingers.

"Seems like something most people think of often."

"I don't," I said.

"Why?"

"Because love hurts."

She smiled, stretching her legs to the dashboard.

"Of course, it does," she replied.

"That's what makes it so good."

At least for one moment in your day

I hope I cross into your thoughts

You are the last thing I see before I go to sleep. I think about how you looked and what you said. I think about the day we shared and moments we connected.

I know I overthink too much, like my mind is the sky and it explodes and rains stardust. I know I can be insecure, like I am always staring in the mirror and seeing another. But I will love you wholly. I will think of you often. I will make you feel like the sun, never ever forgotten.

She said her favorite color was purple, and now I haven't seen purple the same since. I see lavender and think of her, I see her bedroom walls and dream of her, I wear purple t-shirts to feel her around me, I write love letters in purple crayon, because she makes my heart wild and carefree.

I know life doesn't play out like the movies. But I want a happy ending with you.

If your mind needs repairing

Mental illness is not weakness. It doesn't define you. It will try to dictate your days and make you feel cursed. But just like anyone else, you are equally a child of the universe.

If your child says "never mind"

do mind

It's easy to shrug things off

as nothing more than puberty

But being invested

can save a life

They need you

even if sometimes it feels

they don't

Imagine the day as your stage and you are the sun. In the early morning when you rise above the horizon, the light is faint. But as the morning moves forward and the day goes on, the light gets stronger and stronger until it fills the sky.

Your light will get stronger as the day goes on.

Please believe this

As easily as the sun rises

You are enough

In the middle of winter, she walks the street alone, leaving footprints in the snow on her way home. She wonders where she belongs, if she really fits in. But when the sun comes out, the snow melts away. Hold on to your beliefs; stay for the start of a new day.

Life is a conductor, and you are running your hands along an instrument in an orchestra so big it's easy to get lost among the strings and the notes. But a beautiful sound is never lost in a crowd.

Who you are is louder than you think.

The mountain is to climb, not to carry on your shoulders.

They say if you practice something again and again you will become good at it. So why, if you tell yourself every day that you are capable, do you not believe it?

We wish to have more nights where signs come to us like fireflies lighting our path in the right direction. Sometimes darkness settles for long periods of time. But there is reason to darkness, and in some moments, we can find our path even without the light.

Maybe after all this time you were looking to the wrong person to save you. The right person had been there in front of you. You had just forgotten to look in the mirror.

There is bravery in uncertainty.

But in order to leap forward, you need to stop looking back.

It's okay to take a break from the path. You can retreat, heal, and continue your journey when you feel stronger.

Despite all reasons to lock yourself away, fresh air is good for you. Soothing, deep breaths of fresh air. Nature knows what is best for you. So, when the mountains call, don't ignore them.

How many people have you told "it doesn't matter," when really it broke you into a million pieces?

Words look different on pages than in your mind. On pages, they sit quietly, waiting to be read. But inside your head, they're screaming, angry, hurting, bleeding red.

You're so well put together, confident and free. I wonder what it's like to love yourself. But then again, what would I know, maybe you're just like me.

People want to believe in magic, to be wild at heart. They want to see the world in only happiness. But balance requires pain to be part of our lives. Live through the pain, even when it plagues your mind.

I feel sadness when it slips into the sleepy parts of my life. It shows when I don't pick up the pile of clothes on my floor or call back the person I love most. But I recognize it now, I see it, and I fight back.

You might meet someone who will fight harder than anyone to keep you here. But at the end of the day, the battle is still yours. No matter how much someone loves you, they can't win the battle for you.

The mind can be full of dark thoughts. A long hallway, full of compartments. And you push all the bad memories into drawers, trying to make them disappear. Only you know they won't. They'll resurface every time something happens to remind you.

Healing feels like it slips through my fingers sometimes. It is there one minute and then gone with the wind.

But if you need to cry all night,

then cry

If you need to scream into the air,

then scream

If you cannot leave the house,

stay in bed

If you cannot use words,

don't speak

You do not have to show your face

to the world every single day.

You are allowed a day off.

Sadness feels like a lifelong friend some days. As though I cannot let it go, because I am not sure who I would be without it.

Self-Care for the Mind

Think of a positive thought
Remind yourself,
you are capable
Take a walk
Remind yourself,
you are worth each step
Focus on your breathing
and remind yourself,
you are worth each step

In a different universe, maybe I am someone who cannot express how I am feeling. Maybe I am someone with a mind who feels out of control. Maybe I am someone who hears a voice that repeatedly says, "You cannot do this." Which is why, in this universe, I listen to others.

It is messy unlearning who you are

It isn't clean or straightforward

There are ups and downs

There are twists and turns

There are days you feel unheard

But there is beauty in beginning again

Starting over in a new day

Creating a better you, for a better way

I'm learning to love myself, especially the thoughts in my mind. I'm learning that sometimes I will have dark thoughts and other times I won't, and both are okay, as long as I remember I am always worth it.

You told me that what we had wasn't enough

so you turned around and walked away

You left me in pieces with a broken heart

now there are so many reasons I don't trust

anyone who says they want me forever

Because you caught me off guard

and I fell so hard

I couldn't pick myself up off the ground

You said we had something special

but you're a liar

and now I'm waiting here alone

trying to forget your smile helped me breathe

trying to forget you were all I needed

Someone has the headlights on in the drive

And I forget myself every time I close my eyes

It's about being understanding. Even if you are unsure why or don't feel the same things too. Even if you can't predict the triggers or relate to the trauma. It doesn't mean you can't be understanding. Not everyone can say, "Me too," but sometimes the greatest act of kindness is to say

I understand, and I support you.

You will find strength in the everyday moments

Like when your mind aches from all the thoughts

but someone texts to ask how your day is

It's important to have a support network

to be surrounded by people who will listen

It's important to wake up each day and remind yourself

you will get through it one deep breath at a time

There is nothing beautiful

about wishing

you'd never been born

There is nothing poetic

about believing

you are a burden

There is nothing sadder

than thinking

you're ruining the lives

of the people you love

But there is nothing

stronger than you

I am in awe of the way you live

even with all these dark thoughts

You are brave in the way

you begin again each day

Some nights it's as though the moon has fallen, and she is throbbing in my chest. It's as though she is crying out for me to follow the stars, but I cannot see through all the darkness. But then I think of you, and how you said you wouldn't forget to call. How it was past midnight and I began to believe you were just another someone, breaking promises. Only for my phone to ring, and it was your name checking in.

You don't need grand gestures or flowers every day. But when she's had a hard week, and her mind feels like it's shattered into a million pieces, sometimes it's just nice if you take her out for dinner.

Words become trapped in your mind if you don't free them. Write them down, speak them, share them. Even if nobody reads the words or hears the words. They need to be freed.

Let the words go, my friend.

Loneliness comes from getting lost in your own thoughts

and not knowing which way will bring you home

It's important to keep reminding yourself of the moment

Each one is different

Each one passes

But bring yourself back to the present

In every deep breath our mind becomes clearer

Suddenly you notice the light in the curves of her neck

and the coolness of the fresh air

Pause and Reflect

Divinity is seeing colors for how they really are
It's loving for the mind and not the body
It's opening yourself up to every possibility
Being in the moment gives you power
over your own emotions
It says to your mind
you can break
But I will not let you

I'd take your hand all through the seasons, just to remind you that you can make it. Even if every other reason in your life suggests you might not see the morning. I wish I could reach you in the moments you believe it's too late and the world may disappear.

Just hold on; I'm here for you.

Allow your mind to grow

and expand in any way it wants to

You are not broken or damaged beyond repair

You are a warrior

made from ghosts of all the people you've been

Your mind deserves calm waters

Reach for every moment

If your mind has doubts

Self-Doubt

I am only here because there are still parts of you yet to be welcomed. I am sorry for the sweaty palms and your heart beating loudly in your chest. I am sorry if sometimes I stop you from doing your best. I manifest in the moments you take for granted so that you will eventually realize you have what it takes.

Words still hang in my throat

Quivering

Afraid to speak out into the night

But I am reminded

that I am fit to fight

the war

between my head and heart

Because while the world was sleeping

I was tearing myself apart

Sometimes I wonder if fear is really the ghosts inside us

of the things we should have said

but didn't

Self-doubt will hold you down in the way gravity keeps us on earth. To walk alongside this doubt is to learn to live with it and succeed anyway.

I scrawled all my fears into

the sand

But the ocean washed them

away

And I wish it were that easy

That fear disappeared

with the tide

each day

If I were the sun, I'd ask you to write your fears and worries on a note and hand it to me in the late afternoon. I would set and take your fears with me and bury them deep in the moon. Yet the earth is far too big and I am only a person, but your fears are nothing to be ashamed of. Like the sun and the moon, you will never be a burden.

It is not spending endless days with you

that I am afraid of

Because my heart was committed

the moment I saw you

It's handing over my hopes

and dreams

to someone who has the power to drop them

I am not afraid of spiders

or small spaces

or missing flights

I am afraid of

ignoring warning signs

and red flags

and finding out I was right

Despite all my fear

there has never been

a moment of sorrow

when you weren't there

I hear your heart

how it beats against

your chest

I hear you breathe

loud breaths

within your rib cage

Why are you afraid

to listen to your fears

When I've been listening

all along

I remember those moments back in the summer
we sat so close our thighs touched.
So close
I could see the freckles across your nose.

I remember thinking of you in colors
bright and bold.
I remember forgetting all the ideas of love
I had ever been told.

We'd reached and locked hands, timid
not knowing what to say.
Other than,
Can I kiss you?
Can I kiss you for the rest of the day?

I could have spent eternity planting courage in our minds
because in that moment our fears didn't hold us back
and that moment was divine.

It's hard being young. Being a soul growing into its skin. Not knowing if certain feelings are normal or who to let in. When you walk the hallways and your knees shake and you are not sure what to do with all the leftover ache. Things change and people leave. Life feels like you are standing on the edge with a loud heartbeat and dreams impossible to achieve. There will be days you are afraid to live, where your lungs feel hollow and each moment takes all the strength you can give. But it's okay to feel these things, it's okay to make mistakes so that you can grow. You have not failed on the days you draw the curtains across your window.

There are many things I have been

broken

defeated

afraid

but more than that, I have proven to be

bold

strong

brave

Sometimes being alone is too much to face. When everyone keeps telling you to be strong but when you close the bedroom door you're barely hanging on. The days and weeks feel so heavy sometimes, the world becomes a cruel place to be. It makes you lose will, lose focus. And sometimes the road is covered in fog and to step inside is scarier than to just give up.

But you don't need to be afraid, because you are more than enough.

It all matters when you are scared

Maybe there is something you need to say

but you aren't sure how

Maybe there's somewhere you need to be

but you aren't sure how to get there

Maybe there is someone you need to love

but their heart is elsewhere

And it will feel like your chest might explode

and the night is too dark to walk the road

But the fear makes it all valid

The fear makes it important

Don't become so afraid to write how you feel that you lose your love to hold the pen.

It's a fear of telling people everything inside you

because you are afraid it's too ugly for them to hear

You are afraid it will ruin them to know

But each day you stay silent

it's ruining you

They can't face the fear for you

It's your battle

Fight it well

Fight it with anger and with grace

You have spent all these years building a list of the things you can't stand about yourself. You have been trying to hide the deepest parts of you because you are afraid of someone getting close. But there are only so many seasons you can spend with locks on your door. Because eventually someone will walk in and they will want to know you more and more.

There are many things you should care about

Like sick animals, dying trees, and saving the bees.

What others think of you

is not one of these things.

People heal in different ways.

There is no shame in letting someone know you are hurting.

If you are honest, you could spare them some pain too.

The past does not define you. There will be people who once knew you intimately, but they don't know you now. They may remember a chapter that once spoke to them, but they don't get to know the chapters that are coming. You get to write those.

There is power in not being afraid to break.

She wandered into the forest

A crown of flowers in her hair

and the trees whispered

"She has returned"

Spring

A light in the darkness

of the woods

A message of hope

Sometimes life feels like the last step on a ladder, falling into nothing. It feels like moments explode into fragments and force your heart to disappear. You are filled with a feeling of wanting one more chance, just one last day to live every wish unfilled. And when your heart is racing and your feet don't feel planted on the ground, remember falling from the ladder, that deafening silent sound.

We fear losing friends. We fear losing a shoulder to cry on, someone to laugh with, someone who knows our secrets. Someone who has seen us at our best and worst. We fear losing a friend whom we once relied on.

More than that, we fear the reason they left.

What if it was our fault?

It isn't saying "I love you"

People often say these words as freely

as a river runs after the rain

It's whether we'll hear the words back

That's what makes us afraid

Every survivor has different fears

You don't get to choose what should and shouldn't haunt them

Remind Your Daughter

Don't be afraid to speak

Move forward, not backward

Be kind to your changing body

Let your wings spread far and wide

Fall in love even when it brings you to tears

Live courageously alongside your deepest fears

Bravery is baring your soul even when you are met with despair.

We fear the things we don't understand

We fear feelings we have never felt

concepts we have never heard of

We fear the unknown

and the things we have

never dreamed of

Every once in a while, you need to be reminded that flowers wilt in the dark. If you close yourself off to beautiful things, your petals will cease to grow. And with every step back, your hands grasped tightly around your throat, the stems will begin to choke. Flowers need light and love and air. Come back to these things. You need to breathe for life to be spared.

It's not my intention to hold you back. But rather to push you to excel. And I am sorry if sometimes I push too hard. If in the middle of the night you lie awake worrying about the day to come. But after me comes faith and strength to do all that must be done.

Sincerely, Fear

I've tried to send all the doubts into the darkness. But I'm starting to believe that the darkness has been sitting inside me. It grows from the negativity I allow to well inside.

Some days I will come home and I might not say a word. I won't want to talk or be held or tell you about my day. But it doesn't mean I don't love you. It doesn't mean you aren't the sun on a dull, cloud-filled day. It just means I am tired. It means my mind has been giving me grief and I'm exhausted today, and that's okay.

How many people choose not to speak because they are afraid of what others will think?

With every swallowed word, I am feeding the doubt within my soul. If only I could swallow the sun and flowers and force the light back in.

My mind repeats all the mistakes I've made, like a bad movie reminding me of all the things that cause me so much doubt.

There are things that go wrong in my life, like a roller coaster that twists and bends. People say that this is just how life goes. But too often I am wondering if maybe it's just me. Too often I am thinking about how often my doubt shows.

If your mind needs inspiration

Nobody else can tell you how to live your journey, what motivates you, what brings inspiration into your mind. It will be hard to find some days, and on others it will flourish. It is your inner child, inner peace, a reason for you to wake up each day.

There were all these pieces split and broken on the floor, and she spent days on end trying to put the pieces back together again. But if she only realized that life is meant not to restore what was but rather to create something new and move forward.

I see no crime in a well-earned nap

The mind needs rest

"They have good vibes"

Don't shrug this off

Vibes are a necessity

Vibes are important

Especially the good ones

Look for them

Keep them

Genuine people are hard to find

We want to make a difference. We want our art, our music, and our words to have impact. We want our own lives to change others, to matter. So we can leave a legacy, leave something behind that makes every orbit around the sun worth it. It takes great patience to realize we already have. Just by living we have changed the course of someone's life.

Just by existing we have altered someone else's day.

Darling soul, some of life's richest moments come from the ability to laugh at yourself. We make errors; we blunder in the things we do. But this will never give another person the right to humiliate you.

There is no punch line in who you are.

No joke that could ever be made at the expense of your life.

If someone seeks to embarrass you, they are taking it too far.

It doesn't matter to me how many people see these words. All that matters is that they reach the person who needs them most at the right time.

If anything, think of the sky when she falls asleep, how she becomes lavender and apricot and all things sweet.

In the early morning, the sun is rising to the middle of the sky, and I can hear the rustle of the leaves as they whisper to each other. The birds are awake, singing hymns in the trees, and I am reminded of the fortune it is to live on this earth. And even if there are times I have lost my way, this will never waver or denounce my worth.

We spend a lifetime with our feelings; try not to hurt those of others.

You are more than the dust

resting on your windowsill

You are a beacon of light

with dreams to fulfill

You are the wind

rushing forward to bright

new things

You are a summer day

and all the joy it brings

Mistakes do not define you

lessons are to be discovered

And often when you read poetry

there is a little bit of magic

uncovered

Just because the soil is rotten doesn't mean nothing will grow.

Ideas sprout from places once forgotten.

Flowers bloom in spaces that aren't always common.

Dignity is sacred. There will be people who try to strip this from you. Who leave your emotions on the floor and your soul naked and exposed. And instead of the thorns protecting the rose, they will turn on you, cut deep into all that you are trying to be. But they will not crush you. Don't surrender your dignity.

Thoughts grow by investing time and energy into them
words cannot hurt you if you ignore them

You are fire running through open plains

You are thunder, loud and heavy when it rains

You are a hundred miles per hour

and the softest breeze

You are every flower and the tallest of trees

Life runs through you as it does the earth

Take some time to see your worth

You deserve every now and then

To put yourself first

Consistency is one of life's many challenges. To overcome temptation and stay focused on your own path is just a concept to some. But the key comes from within. Start with being consistent with your consistency.

People go against the current every day. Somewhere in the world another person is taking a leap of faith. Someone is choosing to be brave and rise against their fears. Someday you'll be one of those people too. The river doesn't always stay the same. Your time will come.

Of all the ways to break and bend the truth

it was believing you and I were bulletproof

And now I lie awake each night

wondering if I will ever feel again

the way you made me feel

Change is a part of life

How you let it affect you

Will determine how you live

Pain will always be in your life. You need to walk beside it, hold its hand, understand that while it's not always fair, you will learn something from it being there.

Practice forgiveness.

This does not mean you need to forget.

But you do need to forgive to heal yourself.

Sunlight is important, draw the curtains, sweep away the dust.

Build your kingdom the way you want it. The love of your life will not take over or force you to surrender it. Instead they will merge their kingdom with yours.

The grass is not always greener on the other side. Ask yourself, "Why is my grass dying?"

There is no need to lose yourself

to get closer to someone else

Speak honestly, even if it hurts

Leap, even if you are afraid to fall

You are not who you were yesterday or the year before. So when you start to feel helpless and things will not get better, just remember you are born from valleys and autumn leaves. You are a collection of hymns sung through the trees. You will continue to grow, tomorrow and the year after, through every high and every low.

It is difficult to hit refresh and start again. Reality often reflects your state of mind. It takes strength to renew and start from zero. Nobody else has that power. In your life story, you are your own hero.

There is no manual on how to reach your dreams. You could take fifty steps forward and one hundred steps back.

The goal isn't always to move from one step to the next; it's just to keep going.

You won't feel like climbing mountains every morning. Your body gets tired; your mind needs rest. But if every day you wake and keep moving, no matter how monumental or how small, you are already doing your best.

Just because someone is louder than you and willingly makes their opinions known doesn't mean yours aren't valid. Don't let loud voices stop you from using your own.

You can't control how others act, but you can control how you do. Love in the way you wish to be loved. Give thanks in the way you wish to be thanked. Be kind in the way you wish to see kindness shown to you. Stand up for others in the way you hope others may stand up for you. Action starts with an individual. Act with your best intentions.

Be a better you.

The struggle will end. It might not be tomorrow or the next day, but it will end.

The better place will come one day. All the thoughts in your head won't feel as loud, and each breath won't ache as badly. You will find that life is worth living.

You could be seventeen or seventy-five, and you will still have days when nothing seems right and all you can do is hide. You will have nights when small problems will feel like the end of the world and people you thought you knew will do things you didn't think they were capable of. What matters is not your age or the people who tell you that you can't. It's knowing who you are in the moments they challenge the fact that you are beauty and art.

I wish you sunlight on the days that take longer to pass by. I wish you courage during the moments that make you cry. I wish you power to keep your spirit alive. I wish you persistence to meet the dreams for which you strive. I wish you enough joy and understanding to do all it is you want to do. I wish you softness in all the times that are difficult to get through.

I hope you do more than just survive. I hope you act boldly without apologizing for who you are or the things you love. I hope you make art and listen to songs that make you sing out loud. I hope you discover new places and hidden coffee shops. I hope you fall in love with stories and dance in snowflakes and raindrops. I hope you achieve all your dreams and find the courage to love yourself.

I hope you live.

Hope

I am not what watches you as you pick up all the pieces. I am not what makes excuses for all the bruises. I am what you struggle with every day. I am the role you try to downplay. I am the source of your conflict within yourself. I am what you would rather skip, leave up on your shelf. I am the storm before the reward. I am the battle, force, knife, and sword. I am whom you seek when everything is falling apart. I am the version of you that we both know you have. I am what you need to claw back from everything that turned bad. I am the voice you hear morning, noon, and night, reminding you to get up, keep going, take back your future; it's bright.

Burn trails like you are an unstoppable force

When you fall, get back up

You are more than the failures you have experienced

You have every right to demand more from others,

But you should always demand more from yourself
as well

You don't need to take yourself apart to help other people.
You can't be there for someone else if you disappear.

Remember when you were little and your imagination ran free. The dragon under the stairs and the boiling lava between the sofas. At night, you were an astronaut jumping on your bed under glow-in-the-dark stars. By day, you were climbing mountains, running through jungles, and racing cars. Now you are a little older and you wonder if the imagination will disappear. But hold on to your dreams. Without imagination, the excitement of possibility is lost. There is so much wonder in dreaming. Hold on to your imagination.

These are for your mind

The ground feels solid,

Because when we fall

We hit the ground hard.

But we forget that from the ground

Life grows.

When you fall, the hurt won't last.

You will grow again.

"Where would you go?" she asked.

"That's easy," I replied

"Somewhere my mind doesn't ache so much."

I just hoped you would love me

In the way dry earth loves the rain

I just hoped we could be there for each other

Even after all the years of pain

Trust the universe they say

Things will soon come your way

But sometimes things don't

So maybe it isn't about trusting the universe at all

Maybe it's about trusting yourself

Especially in the moments you fall

Such a large world we live in and an even bigger universe. So many things to ponder. So many places and things to think about, and yet here I am, and all my thoughts are of you.

In her absence my mind feels like an attic

destined to grow dust

between my bones

My thoughts are no more than

boxes piled on top of each other

and my heart is the window

with the shades drawn

Maybe we met when the timing
            wasn't right
You were awfully silent
and in all the quiet
I needed air to fill the spaces
            between my lungs

We thought we were in love
            lost in days
filled with thoughts of each other

But what is love
            where there is no trust
and what is trust
if after that day
I couldn't believe anything else
            you had to say

There are moments, fragments within my life that can make my mind feel like it's been swallowed. As though I am a sinkhole. But then I remind myself what I live for: warm nights, clear skies, to be in the arms of the one I love.

Other people aren't going to give you closure

Despite how badly you want it to come from them

The closure is always going to come from you

Rise the way mountains rose from the ocean

Your voice should not be unheard

Your thoughts should not be erased

Grow and forge ahead

A woman like you

Deserves justice

Timing is such a funny thing

How some things can feel so right

and others so wrong

Even if my mind is a

little cluttered

Somewhere in all the fog

I still think you belong to me

Back then, right now, forever

Only you decide

How your story must be told

Be daring, be bold

The things that terrify us are often the things we can't control

Will I ever find my person?

Will I get that job?

Will it all work out?

Soothe your racing thoughts by reminding yourself

life has a funny way of working out

It doesn't matter if there are days you don't feel like talking, any more than the days you need reassurance. I know you need time for your mind to recharge and your soul to breathe. I am not here to be angry in the moments you feel insecure or the times you question your worth. I am not here to judge you for your mistakes or question your integrity. I'm here to listen to you; I'm here to show you that you can trust me. Hold my secrets and I'll hold yours. Listen to my thoughts and I'll listen to yours.

It's important you keep thinking

      Keep questioning

Don't let your mind become

      full of waste

Let it flourish

Show the world you are a dreamer

a thinker

and not just another face

You always remember your first love

for better or worse

And more often than not, they don't cross your mind

But one day, you'll look up at the sky

and think about how it's the same color

as her eyes

One of the best things about writing is imagination. It's diving into feelings and experiences you may not have had and immersing yourself in a world of wonder. For the people who tell you that you can only write of the things you know—let them stay boring.

Be magic.

It was spring, and I was driving along unfamiliar roads, in a place I had never been. The trees reminded me of unity, all lined up peacefully. I thought about who we all are as people, how we come together in moments we need hope. I thought about how we draw inspiration from each other, how we long to be in love with another. I wondered how many of us have someone else to rely on, what happens when we don't. The nightmares that play over and over again when the days seem like they are running out of hope. And I wanted to stretch my arms out wide, welcome the hopes and dreams of others, nurture them, support them, remind you that things keep moving no matter how strange and difficult the world seems. The trees will continue to line the roads; the sun will shine through the clouds; and despite a very real feeling of doubt, just know that of you, I'll always be proud.

All this time, I've been thinking about happy endings, how destiny is set and maybe this is all it. But then I am reminded that destiny can change; as often as the mountains rumble and sky splits into color, your happy ending could always be right around the corner.

It's difficult to be the best version of yourself all the time. But perhaps life isn't about that. You don't have to always be in a good mood; you don't have to always be sociable or productive. It's about how much you try, even when it feels like life keeps flipping upside down.

Silence can either be devastating or refreshing.

It's really our minds that decide.

I read somewhere once that our minds can blend together in harmony. The mind of a musician who plays music, even while playing as an individual, can synchronize with another musician. As though somehow both their brain waves light up to make the melody. I like to dream that hearts and minds are like this, somehow; we are all different, but we are a harmony.

It's the start of the week, and I am dreaming of the weekend. It feels like so many hours in between, until I get to see you again. My mind is driving me wild with all these thoughts of us, sitting on the beach, beers at our feet, holding hands, and playing music from our phones. When the lights go out, I think about you and me, spending every weekend together for the rest of our lives.

If you asked me if she deserved a second chance, it is likely I'd say no. Not because people don't deserve second chances but because some people are so toxic for your mind it becomes dangerous. And even if I don't want to see her cry, and even if I wish her happiness, the truth is it's hard to know if someone like her will ever be happy. My heart was so heavy, every day after she broke my heart. But it's lighter now, stronger. I can sleep at night without the nightmares. I can look in the mirror without the long questions about my own worth. So, honestly, from the bottom of my heart, I hope I never see her face again.

I was pulling on my shirt, twisting the fabric around my
fingers, staring at my feet; I was nervous, and you knew it.

"Why are you nervous?"

"It's you," I said. "You make me nervous."

And this smile split across your face, and you started to play
with your hair.

"Funny," you replied. "You make me nervous too."

Corner of the World

There is a place I call home, and sometimes it feels like a quiet little corner of the world. It is where I live and breathe and scrawl my feelings on pages. It is where I cry and let down my walls on the days I've come up empty and all I do is fall. This corner, filled with comfort and the ones I love, filled with friendship and ideas always churning, a fire always burning. Each time I venture from this place, to board planes and take roads I never dreamed possible, all I have to do is close my eyes and think how safe I feel when I'm here. The light is always on, the kettle always warm, a dog always asleep at my feet. This corner of the world where I never feel alone.

It is my home.

When I close my eyes, I am flying. I am a rocket, taking off into the sky. I am the earth, orbiting the sun. I am a comet, blazing through darkness littered with tiny sparks. Like the doubts in my mind, gravity pulls me, trying to rip me apart. But it's been far too long, and every day I have been growing stronger. I will no longer allow people to bring me down. I will defy the odds; I will keep seeking the universe beyond.

The mind is chaos one moment and calm the next, much like the sea. But my mind will still be thinking about you, even when we're seventy. I've been thinking about our forever, how memories fade but the light in our eyes stays. When we're older, and I stumble over my words, and your dress is a little longer to cover the veins on your ankles, I'll be thinking about the plans we made when we were younger, how you would take me in your arms and kiss me like there was no one else in the room. Darling, I breathe for you; my heart is yours, for every rose that blooms.

So here you are, and you think about someone more than you should. She calls you in the middle of the night and sends you love notes when you need them most. She will arrive on your doorstep with a bottle of wine, and you'll wonder most days, How can she ever be mine? But she disappears as quickly as she comes around, and she leaves you with too many thoughts in your head and a heart that races too often than rests.

I don't believe peace starts with removing all thoughts from your mind. I believe it starts with knowing they'll always be there and learning how to cope.

People are always going to have something to say. Whether it's positive or negative is beside the point. The point is really the fact that you aren't ever going to be able to fully control what they say. But you can control how it affects your thinking. It's important to remind yourself in moments of doubt how you matter and how your existence is important. Despite what people may say or think about you or your art, the most valid and important opinion is your own. Do you love your art? Do you love yourself? What do you think about yourself? And if on some days it takes a little longer to answer, there's no shame in this. The shame comes from the moments you allow small-minded people to control how you think about yourself. Because, really, what a shame it is when you don't believe how truly wonderful you are.

Transformation requires belief. Belief in yourself, belief from others, a will to change what makes you unhappy. Transformation starts in your thinking. What motivates you to do better than the days before. So if you are needing belief to begin—this is it.

I believe you can transform.

Wisdom is not always shutting the world out or eliminating every thought that crosses your mind. It's acknowledging that as much as you will always feel, you will always think too. Wisdom is how to be at ease with this.

Expectations

Often, we grow ideas in our minds of how things should
be. We imagine scenarios, and we dream of the way others
may act. We may do this in relationships or friendships
or opportunities. The trouble with this is the grief we feel
if plans or people don't go or act in the way we expected
them to. The reality in all this is we will probably continue
to envision ideas that never come true or expect others
to respond in ways they never will. But it's important to
understand the grief is valid. The things we thought we knew
may not always be true, but at the time they felt very real. It's
okay to cry about this, to talk about it. As long as, in the end,
you let the expectation go.

Hear your mind, feel your spirit

All your thoughts racing, moving

In the chaos may you find

the things that make you afraid

Hold them, floating, gliding

bring your feet back to the ground

Let your courage now begin

Live the life you've dreamed

Open up your eyes

Only you alone can make

Your thoughts take flight

You can completely shatter more than once in your life, and every time the pieces come together, you'll look a little different, think a little different, and the way you carry yourself may change. But above everything, inside all those pieces is a fire burning. You are more than the moments your eyes sparkle, more than the days a cloud hangs above your head. You are capable of building yourself again.

If only we all had a map of our mind. Full of paths to take and signs leading us in the right direction. But sometimes becoming lost in the woods is a good thing. It teaches us about the way we think, how deeply we can wonder about life's meaning. It teaches us about the conversations we truly seek.

Your mind can take you to places your body cannot. It's important to grow your thinking, to expand what you know. Just because someone else thinks they have all the answers doesn't mean they do. You can change your mind, reinvent yourself a hundred different times. The gift you give yourself is knowing when to breathe and knowing when to climb.

Your mind will always try to convince you it knows best. That it knows more than the heart and the soul. But sometimes the mind forgets that each part works together, as a whole.

Thank you for reading this book.

I hope you enjoyed reading it as much as I enjoyed writing it.

You can view more of my work on Twitter @CourtPeppernell and Instagram @courtneypeppernell.

Feel free to write to me via courtney@pepperbooks.org.

Pillow Thoughts app now available worldwide for free download on all iOS and Android devices. Download yours today through the app store!

Pillow Thoughts III

Andrews McMeel Publishing
a division of Andrews McMeel Universal
1130 Walnut Street, Kansas City, Missouri 64106

www.andrewsmcmeel.com

19 20 21 22 23 BVG 10 9 8 7 6 5 4 3 2 1

ISBN: 978-1-4494-9705-7

Library of Congress Control Number: 2018959583

Editor: Patty Rice
Designer, Art Director: Diane Marsh
Production Editor: Elizabeth A. Garcia
Production Manager: Cliff Koehler

Illustrations by Ryan Gerber

ATTENTION: SCHOOLS AND BUSINESSES
Andrews McMeel books are available at quantity discounts
with bulk purchase for educational, business, or sales
promotional use. For information, please e-mail the
Andrews McMeel Publishing Special Sales Department:
specialsales@amuniversal.com.